ART FROM WOOD

with projects using branches, leaves and seeds

Gillian Chapman & Pam Robson

Wayland

SALVAGED!

Art from Fabric
Art from Packaging
Art from Paper
Art from Rocks and Shells
Art from Sand and Earth
Art from Wood

This book was prepared for Wayland (Publishers) Ltd
by Globe Education, Nantwich, Cheshire

Artwork and design by Gillian Chapman
Photography by Rupert Horrox

First published in 1995 by
Wayland (Publishers) Ltd
61 Western Road, Hove
East Sussex BN3 1JD

Printed and bound by
G. Canale & C. S. p. A., Turin

British Library Cataloguing in Publication Data

Chapman, Gillian
Art from Wood. – (Salvaged series)
I. Title II. Robson, Pam III. Series
745.51

ISBN 0 7502 1528 3

Acknowledgments

Special thanks to KC for his help in making the projects.
Photographs on p. 4 Robert Harding,
on p. 5 top Tony Stone/Sister Daniel,
and on p. 5 inset The Grizedale Society.

Contents

Our Precious Forests

Deforestation

Deforestation is one of the many environmental problems that could threaten the future of our planet. People use up Earth's limited natural resources – millions of trees are cut down for their timber or to provide land for farming. Forests are a vital part of the global ecosystem supporting millions of species of animals and plants. Their destruction causes ecological harm and contributes to climatic change.

Rain forest is disappearing at a tremendous rate every day.

Agenda 21

In 1992, world leaders met in Rio de Janeiro for an Earth Summit. Together they agreed a plan known as Agenda 21. This is to help save Planet Earth. The tree of life is its symbol. Trees are the lungs of our planet, yet one square kilometre of rain forest is destroyed every minute. Agenda 21 asks us to keep this to a minimum by using discarded trees and reusing old timber.

A Throw-away Society

We live in a throw-away society that wastes the limited natural resources of the Earth. This book suggests ideas for recycling wood and tree litter that help conserve the world's forests and support Agenda 21.

The Tree of Life

In ancient times, trees were worshipped as a source of power. People believed that by making use of bark and foliage the spirit of the trees could be captured. The tree of life features in the folk art of many cultures, particularly Mexico. In West Africa, some flags carry tree of life images.

Deer sculpture made by Sophie Ryder from twigs in Grizedale Forest in Cumbria, northern England.

Greek Mythology
The ancient Greeks believed that trees were inhabited by their gods. Wood nymphs, or Dryades – the daughters of Zeus – were said to come to life with each new tree and, eventually, to die with it.

Ancient Trees
The oldest living trees began their growth over 4,000 years ago. Tree life spans vary according to each species. Many trees have seen centuries of history which is now recorded in their growth rings. At the same time trees have supported ecosystems of flora and fauna that have survived for generations.

Materials from Trees
Trees provide food, fuel and shade. They act as wind breaks and hold the soil, preventing erosion. Trees transpire, taking in carbon dioxide and sending water vapour and oxygen into the air. From trees we obtain wood to make paper, rubber, cork and kapok. Some vital medicines also come from trees.

Storm Damage
Storm winds can devastate forests and woodlands – hurricanes can uproot trees. Storm-damaged wood is often left to rot or it is burned. Such materials can be used for purposeful projects.

Tree Litter
Trees constantly shed bark, leaves, fruits or seeds. Healthy seeds mean more trees will grow. The most purposeful project that you can carry out is to plant a tree.

Pattern and Texture

Design in Nature
The natural world is a source of inspiration to artists and scientists alike. In it we find harmony of shape and design. In nature we can see symmetry, pattern and proportion – look closely at the form of a pine cone.

Observing and Collecting
Observe the natural world of woodland or forest. Look at lines, patterns and shapes, feel the different textures. Collect leaves, seeds and pieces of wood and bark from the forest floor. Do the lines on a piece of bark look like ripples on water?

Arrange your collection in simple patterns, according to shape and colour. Use a flat surface, outdoors if possible, as a background for your pattern making.

Natural Materials for Projects

Preserving Materials
Natural materials all begin to wither and decay as soon as they fall from the trees. Seeds, bark and pieces of wood last longer if stored in a cool, dry place.

Leaves will start to lose their colour immediately. Coating them in melted, but not boiling, wax will help them to keep their colours. You can stand bunches of leaves and grasses in a glycerine solution, one part glycerine to two parts hot water. Leave them for a few days to absorb the glycerine.

Withered and Preserved Leaves

Seasonal Materials

Natural materials are seasonal. They are found only at certain times of the year. Leaves can only be collected during autumn, or, in the tropics, during the dry season. If you live in the temperate regions of the southern hemisphere, autumn occurs when the north is enjoying spring. In the tropics there are two seasons – wet and dry. The weather also affects all natural materials. Collect them on dry, sunny days from the ground around the tree. Do not break anything from a living tree.

Simple Patterns using Natural Materials

Photographs of Natural Patterns

Temporary Patterns

Throughout time, craftspeople have made patterns using natural materials. These simple works of art are often of a spiritual nature and are meant to be temporary. Today, many artists carry on this tradition and place their artwork in a chosen environment where it is left to be blown away by the wind and rain – the only record possibly being a photograph. You can take photographs of your leaf and seed patterns to keep as a record.

7

Collage Shapes

Colour, pattern and texture all play an important part in the design of a collage. The natural materials themselves may suggest a picture. Look carefully at all the objects in your tree litter collection. Do any of them have a shape that suggests something to you? Sycamore seeds may remind you of a pair of ears. Some leaves make a 'hand' shape. Look at the cockerel's tail in the collage below. Plan your design first. Either sketch it on a sheet of paper or draw directly on to the backing board.

Collage Pictures

All collage work is best stuck on to a rigid surface. Your design may look better on a coloured or textured background. Before glueing anything down, position your materials by moving them round to find the best arrangement. PVA glue is best for lightweight materials, such as leaves, twigs and seeds. A diluted solution of PVA and water will make a glaze that can be applied to the finished collage. This will help to preserve the natural materials so they do not decay.

Plan Design First

Cockerel Collage

Collage Materials

Collages and Frames

Natural Glues

Whenever possible use water-based, environmentally-friendly glues. In the forests you can see examples of natural glues. For example, pine trees produce a sticky sap to protect damaged branches. This sap eventually becomes amber and often contains the bodies of trapped insects. Spiders build sticky webs as food traps. Wasps' nests are held together with a papier mâché substance the wasps create from chewed wood.

Making a Picture Frame

A collage picture will look even better displayed within a natural collage frame. Make a frame from rigid card, cutting out a 'window' slightly smaller than the picture. The frame should be 10 cm all round and the window will cover the rough edges of the collage. Hinge a piece of backing card to the top of the frame and attach the picture to it, allowing the frame to fold over and cover the edges neatly. Now the framed collage can be hung on the wall.

Collage Walks

All the materials you need to make natural collages are freely available. In towns and cities, you can look in parks and gardens – even on grass verges. In the countryside, you can look in hedgerows and woodland as well. Here are some ideas for displaying and recording the finds of a nature walk.

Footprint Collage

This is a collage of materials found underfoot whilst walking through a park or forest. All kinds of interesting leaves, twigs and seeds make up the collage including pieces of litter. Draw a large human or animal footprint first on stiff card. Then arrange your materials within the shape. When you are pleased with the design glue everything down firmly.

Footprint Collage

Walk in Time

The scale along the bottom records the time in minutes.

Walk in Time

If you are planning a long walk through forest or parkland, make a record of your progress as you walk along collecting materials. Keep a note of the time, the weather and the type of countryside you are walking through. When you return home, arrange your collection on a horizontal strip of card together with your notes. You may like to sketch or paint the landscape as a background to the collage.

Long Walks

Your collection can also be arranged on a vertical strip. Glue or thread each item on paper or fabric, arranging them in the order in which you found them. If the walk went uphill, the natural changes will be apparent through the items collected.

When you are walking in the countryside, think about why you are attracted to certain materials. What makes you select and pick up one leaf or stone and not another similar one? Is it a particular shape or colour that appeals? When you are sorting and cleaning the materials at home, again you will use some, but discard others. Think carefully about why you make your choices.

Long Walks

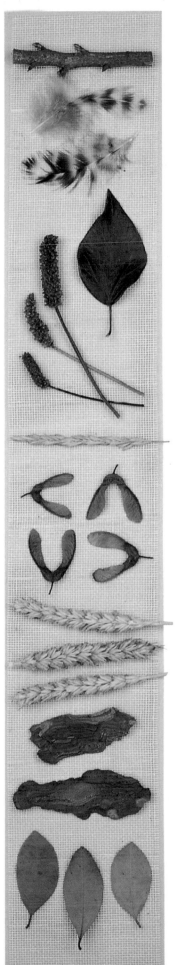

Found Objects

Sculpture from Found Objects

An artist using found objects to create works of art is both a collector and creator. Found art describes art created almost entirely from a natural found object. The artist is guided by the natural shape of the object. While you are out walking in the woods or along a beach, look out for some interesting pieces of wood. Does the shape suggest anything to you? A branch may have a texture that resembles animal fur. A piece of wood may have a strange, weathered shape. You could also smooth pieces of wood with sandpaper and carve them into shapes.

Bark Jigsaw

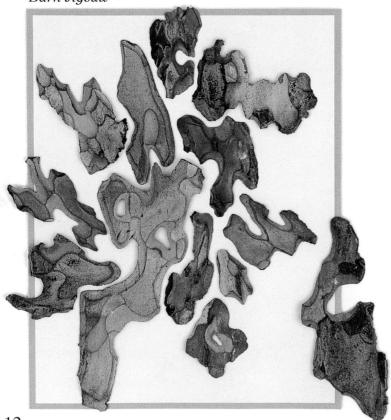

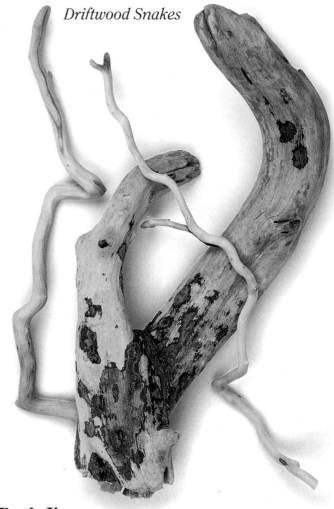

Driftwood Snakes

Bark Jigsaws

Tree bark is a hard, protective layer of dead tissue. As a tree grows, the bark around the trunk cracks and becomes deeply furrowed. Each species of tree has its own distinctive bark pattern. Some trees shed their bark and this can be collected, but never strip bark from a living tree or the tree will die. Bark comes in a variety of colours, textures and thicknesses. Look around the foot of a pine tree, you may find some bark sections. Try matching them up to create a bark jigsaw.

*Branch
Collage*

Branch Collage

Ask an adult to saw a small branch into cross-sections for you. Observe the growth rings inside each section. Arrange the pieces on a wooden background to make a branch collage.

*Joining Bundles
of Twigs*

Twig Animals

Hedges and some trees are pruned regularly. The discarded cuttings can be used to make animal shapes. Choose long, flexible twigs and strip off any leaves. Bind the bundles of twigs together with string or raffia, adding smaller bundles for limbs. Features such as ears, eyes and whiskers can be made from smaller twigs, seeds and pine needles.

Twig Animal

Tools to make Marks

Ancient Crafts

Long ago, the use of tools separated humans from other animals. The first simple tools may have been sticks found amongst tree litter. The Aboriginal dreamtime story pictures were first recorded on bark and stone using sticks and fibres as tools. The ends were frayed or had hairs or feathers attached. American Indians in the south-west of North America softened the ends of yucca stalks by chewing – the stalks were used as brushes to paint pottery.

Tools to Work With

Look around amongst tree litter to find twigs and dried seed heads suitable to use as pattern-making tools. Make brushes by tying dried grasses, feathers or pine needles to twigs. Push thistle heads into hollowed elder wood handles. Experiment with a range of natural materials. Each will make a different mark. Cut a design into the cross-section of a twig. Look for sticks of charcoal amongst a burned-out bonfire and try drawing with them.

dried grasses

dried seed head

squashed twig

pine needles

feathers

charcoal

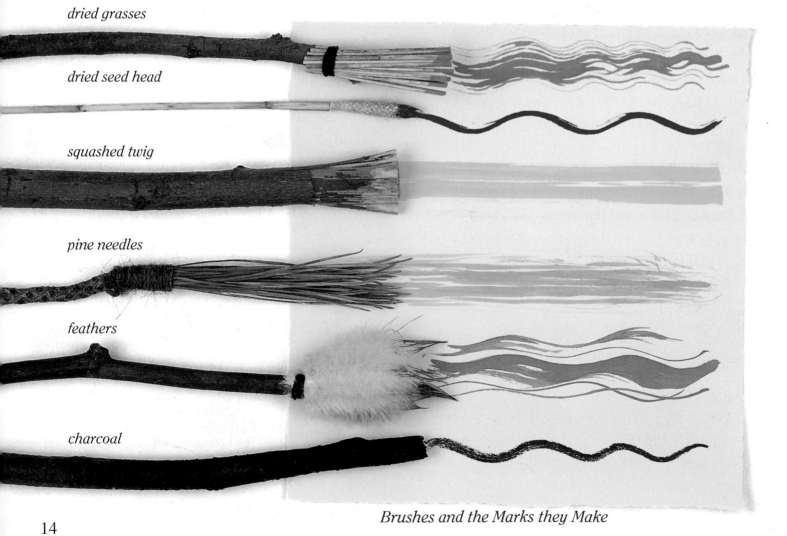

Brushes and the Marks they Make

Bark Painting

Stone Painting

Surfaces to Work Upon

Early peoples worked on bark and foliage in the belief that the power of the tree then passed to them. The Fijians made a bark cloth called tapa on which patterns were stamped with leaves and bamboo tubes dipped in dye. The Aztecs made paper from bark. Use your handmade brushes to make patterns on bark and stone.

Natural Pigments

Charcoal powder and natural pigments of ground ochre and clay were probably used to create the famous stone age cave paintings of spotted horses found at Pech-Merle in France.

Charcoal is made by burning wood inside a container that keeps it short of air. The best kind of wood is obtained by coppicing trees. This involves cutting back small areas within woodland, allowing sunlight to enter and letting young trees grow. Coppicing is good for the environment because it encourages ecosystems to thrive.

Twig Tool Container

Make a twig container to store your tools by cutting down a plastic bottle and covering it with twigs. Hold the twigs in place with tape while working but bind them together with string to finish.

Printing Sticks

Twig Tool Container

15

Rubbings and Stencils

Tree Types

A tree can be identified by its bark. Bark
is the tree's armour against the elements.
It protects the living tissue beneath from
the weather, insects and even fire. It is
found in an amazing variety of colours
and textures. Some insects bore into the
bark creating distinctive marks. As strips
of old bark peel off, new bark is revealed
growing underneath. On a redwood tree
the bark may be 30 cm thick.

Making a Leaf Rubbing

Book of Rubbings

Bark and Leaf Rubbings

By taking bark rubbings from a wide
variety of trees, you can discover much
about different textures. Rubbings can
also be made using leaves. Choose
leaves that have a distinctive shape and
prominent veins. Make your rubbing
with a wax crayon on light-coloured
paper using the reverse side of the leaf.
Take bark and leaf rubbings from the
same tree and make a book to keep a
record of your best rubbings. Label and
date your work, putting bark and leaf
rubbings from the same tree together.

Natural Templates

Leaves come in so many shapes and sizes that they all make perfect natural templates for stencilling and splatter pictures. Choose strong leaves that have a bold shape – sycamore, maple and oak leaves are ideal. Ferns and grasses are interesting, but are too delicate to use.

Splatter Painting

Dip an old toothbrush or nailbrush in paint and stroke the bristles with a stick to make the paint splatter over the leaf stencil. Practise first on scrap paper before you start on a project. Be careful not to allow the paint to become too watery. Build up your design by overlapping the leaf shapes and changing the paint colour. Let each layer of paint dry before adding another, to avoid smudges.

Splatter Scroll

Splatter Lanterns

Splatter Scrolls and Lanterns

Make a series of splatter leaf patterns on a long piece of paper or fabric and turn it into a hanging scroll or banner. Attach the scroll by fixing each end to a branch, then suspend it with string.

Paper decorated with leaf splatter patterns can also be curled around a glass jar, containing a candle. The candle or night light will glow through the printed paper, showing the leaf pattern. This is an unusual way of making lanterns for Hallowe'en.

17

Natural Block Prints

Woodcuts

In the fifteenth and sixteenth centuries woodcut illustrations became popular in Germany. A design was drawn on to a wood block and the parts intended to be white were cut away, leaving the design in relief. Early wood blocks were made from softwood like pear or beech. The block was cut along the wood grain so little detail was possible. Later, wood engravers used hardwood blocks cut across the grain, and more delicate lines could be cut.

Printing Papers

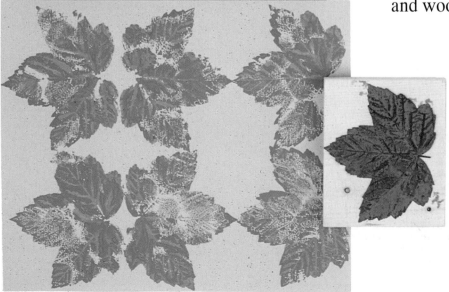

Making Natural Blocks

Instead of carving a design, you can glue a raised pattern on to a wood block. Interesting shapes like leaves, grasses and evergreen twigs are ideal materials to use. Cut blocks of wood that you will find easy to grip from discarded branches. Glue the foliage to the flat surface. Apply paint to the raised design with a brush or roller, then press the block down on to paper. Practise first on scrap paper before starting on a large piece of work.

Seasoned Wood Blocks

Wood from the forest floor contains moisture which makes it weaker and less elastic. Wood from a woodyard has been seasoned, or dried out, making it stronger. Use off-cuts of seasoned wood to make blocks and create relief patterns using scraps of dowel, old matchsticks and wooden cocktail sticks.

Printing Blocks

Making Use of Your Prints

The advantage of a printing block is that a series of repetitive designs can be made and repeated for as long as the block lasts. Blocks are ideal for creating exciting patterns and effects that have many practical applications.

Experiment by painting your printing blocks with different colours and alternating and reversing the blocks to give a range of patterns. The finished printed papers can be used as wrapping papers to cover presents or gift boxes.

If you have a single design that works well, an individual leaf or fern motif, use it to decorate writing paper, labels and envelopes.

Printed papers can also be used to cover and protect your personal books and folders, making them unique.

Printed Giftwrap

Giftbox and Tag

Writing Paper

Envelope and Label

19

Knots and Branches

Wood

Wood is an organic material; it comes from a living tree and has many uses. There are two main types of trees – softwoods such as pine, and hardwoods such as mahogany. Hardwoods take many years to grow to full size.

Willow and yew can be used for basket weaving. Sycamore can be carved. Sailing ships like the *Mayflower* were built from oak. The colour of each type of wood varies – pine and mahogany furniture look very different. Look for the knots in wooden furniture. What causes them?

Polished Wood showing Knots and Grain

Knots

The side branches of a tree make small ring-like markings in the wood. These can only be seen when the wood is cut into plank sections. If you visit a carpenter's workshop or a woodyard look at a variety of seasoned wood planks and observe the knot patterns. Recreate these patterns by drawing knot designs or try taking rubbings of knots in wood. Furniture makers use the knot patterns in wood to make furniture more attractive.

How to Tie Knots

clove hitch

slip knot

reef knot

Knotting Threads

Whenever you use string or thread in craftwork, you will need to tie them together with a secure knot. These diagrams show you how to tie some very useful knots.

Branch Weaving

Branch weaving is an easy introduction to the techniques of weaving. A forked branch acts as a simple loom and threads are bound across. Grasses, leaves, feathers and other natural materials are woven through the threads at random.

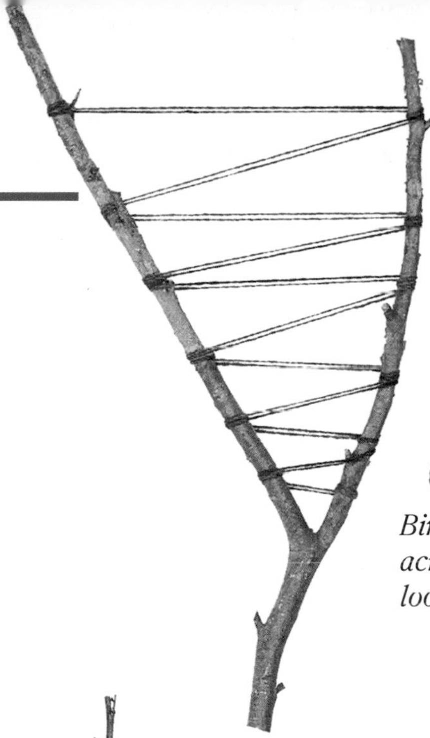

Bind the warp thread across the branch loom.

Choosing Materials

The success of the finished weaving will depend on the choice of the branch loom. At first, a branch with two or three forks is enough. Other branches should be cut off. Tie a length of string or coloured yarn to the top fork and wind it back and forth across the branch, as shown in the diagram. These are the warp threads. Natural materials can now be woven in and out through these threads – over one strand and under the next.

As you get more confident you can experiment with more complex branch looms, threading all kinds of materials into the weaving.

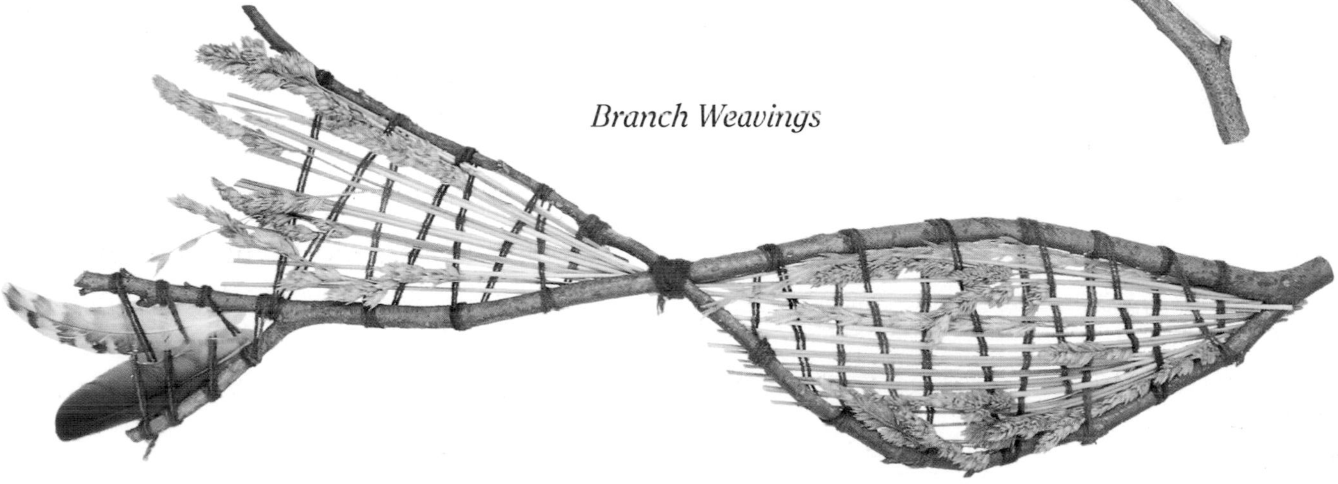

Branch Weavings

Wall Hangings

Weaving from Natural Materials

Using natural materials from forests and woodlands you can create attractive designs.

The North American Indians of the north-west coast relied upon materials from the red cedar tree for their homes, clothing and artefacts. They were able to weave waterproof cloth from bark.

During The Second World War, when supplies of cotton were cut off, the Germans used nettle fibres to weave sand bags for the army. Nettle cloth weaving is used in Nepal today. Perhaps nettle cloth is a fabric of the future.

Making a Loom

Lay Out the Materials on to Scrap Paper First

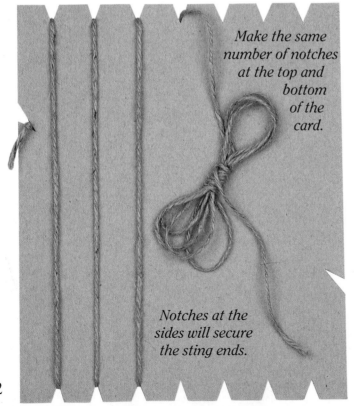

Make the same number of notches at the top and bottom of the card.

Notches at the sides will secure the sting ends.

Planning and Sorting

Making a weaving can be a small individual project or the result of a group working together. As you are using natural materials the finished artefact will be of a temporary nature. Try not to use fresh materials that will shrivel quickly, like green leaves, but choose dry grasses, twigs, seeds and feathers that will last longer.

Sort your natural materials according to texture and colour. Lay them out first on scrap paper, making sure you have plenty to choose from. Plan your design, making it interesting and surprising. Include any unusual items you find.

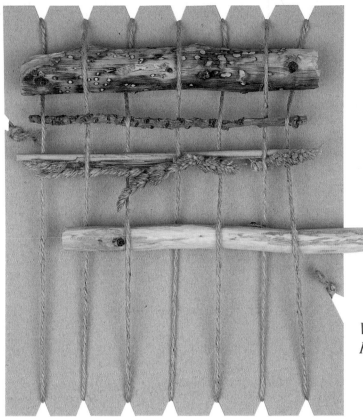

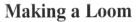

Making a Loom

For most weavings you can use a card loom. Cut a piece of strong card the same size as your design. Make notches along the opposite sides and wind string around them forming the warp threads. Secure both ends of string very firmly because the weaving will be under a lot of tension when you begin working.

Weaving in Progress

Wall Hanging

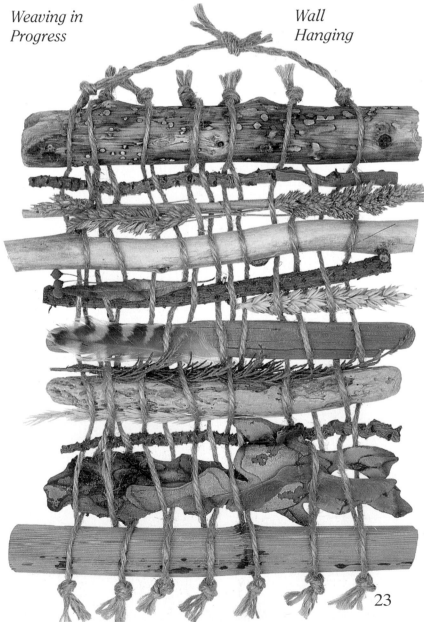

Weaving Materials

Weave long flexible twigs and grasses in and out of the warp threads. Fill in the gaps between thicker pieces of wood with woven string and grasses to help support them. Try to start and finish with a strong piece of wood that stretches right across the weaving.

Removing the Loom

When the weaving is complete you will need to take it off the card. (You may need some help with this stage.)
Cut the warp threads halfway down the card at the back, only two or three at a time. Knot them together, top and bottom, and continue until all threads are knotted. Hang the weaving by the top threads. Try tying pebbles to the bottom threads to make weighted tassels, decorated with seeds and grasses.

23

Leaf Baskets

Why Do Leaves Change Colour?

Deciduous trees shed their leaves in autumn so the trees can survive the winter by conserving water. The green of the leaves is caused by the presence of chlorophyll. As the chlorophyll begins to disappear, the sugars in the leaves create new red, orange and yellow colours.

Leaf Litter

Trees are constantly shedding litter. Leaf litter is the organic matter found on the forest floor. Mixed with the dead leaves are twigs, bark, fruits and seeds and other natural materials. Gradually leaf litter decomposes as it reacts with water, air and minerals to form a layer of new soil. Trees make their own soil by dropping leaves, branches and bark on to the forest floor. This soil provides the necessary nutrients for new trees to grow.

Growing Trees in Leaf Pots

By growing trees from seeds and transplanting the saplings in the right environment, you are helping to preserve the growing cycle. Collect healthy seeds from the forest floor and grow them in leaf pots. Make the leaf pots in the same way as the leaf baskets opposite using plastic flower pots as moulds. When your saplings are strong enough, find suitable places to transplant them in their leaf pots – they could be there for your lifetime.

Coppicing

New growth also needs sunlight. Coppicing not only provides the raw materials for charcoal and other wood products but also allows sunshine to enter dense woodland. In this way new ecosystems are encouraged to develop.

Tree Saplings Growing in Leaf Pots

Leaf Baskets

Leaf baskets are made from leaves moulded together using a water-based adhesive. They do not last long as the natural fibres in the leaves soon break down. Seedlings or plants can be grown in them and later the whole basket can be planted in the ground.

Building up Leaf Layers on a Bowl Mould

Making the Leaf Baskets

Collect together a quantity of leaves. Choose dry, supple leaves of medium-size. They can be arranged on the baskets by shape and colour, but their colour will soon fade. Find a plastic bowl to use as a mould and cover the outside with petroleum jelly. Build up layers of leaves and adhesive as you would papier mâché.

When the layering is finished, leave the basket until completely dry before removing it from the mould. You could try decorating the basket with small seeds.

Leaf Baskets

Animal Houses

Ecosystems

Trees are vital to the survival of forest and woodland ecosystems. Around an oak tree, there is a tightly knit community of plants and animals that rely upon each other for survival. Established food chains exist. Oak moth caterpillars eat the leaves, small birds like blue tits eat the caterpillars, sparrow hawks eat the small birds. In the tree, squirrels eat the acorns and on the ground other tiny mammals feed on the leaf litter.

In tropical rain forests, even more complex ecosystems exist. These disappear daily as huge areas of the forests are destroyed.

How to Make an Animal House

Making an animal house is not as difficult as it seems but you will need an adult to help you use tools like the drill and hammer. Collect together all the scraps and offcuts of wood you can find.

A rough plan for the animal house is outlined here but you may need to adapt it to suit the materials you have. Design the house with a particular creature in mind. It might be a nesting box for wild birds, or a home for a pet mouse or a hamster. Any sawdust and wood shavings can all be kept as bedding material for small animals and birds.

Plan of Construction

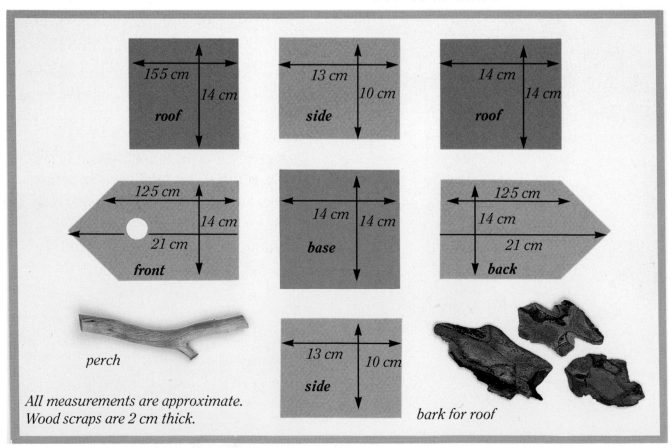

155 cm — roof — 14 cm
13 cm — side — 10 cm
14 cm — roof — 14 cm
125 cm — front — 14 cm — 21 cm
14 cm — base — 14 cm
125 cm — back — 14 cm — 21 cm
perch
13 cm — side — 10 cm
bark for roof

All measurements are approximate.
Wood scraps are 2 cm thick.

Planning the Construction

Using wood, construct a basic box shape with a sloping roof. It will help if you make a plan of the house first. Measure and mark up the wood carefully according to your plan, then get an adult to cut it to size with a saw.

Arrange all the pieces together, making sure they will fit exactly. The size of the entrance must be cut to an appropriate size. To suit blue tits, get an adult to drill the entrance hole in the front piece using a hand drill with a bit about 2·5 cm wide. Make it larger to encourage bigger visitors.

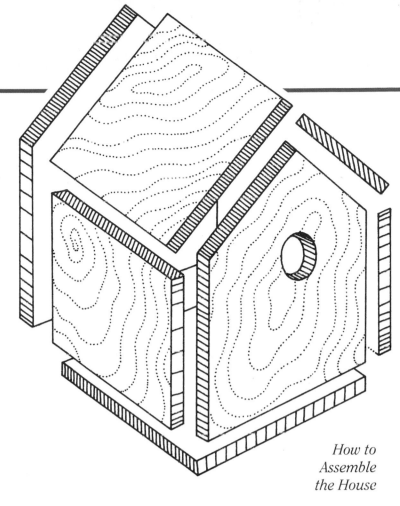

How to Assemble the House

Begin by nailing the sides to the front and back. Then attach the base and finally the roof sections. Use small tacks and be careful with the hammer! One roof section is larger than the other. Overlap them for a neat finish.

Finishing off

Decorate the animal house with pieces of bark on the roof. Nail a twig perch outside the entrance hole if it is for a bird resident. Finally make the house weatherproof by coating it with polyurethane varnish.

Animal House

Making Music

Early Music

The first musical instruments were made from wood. Wood is a resonant material through which sound vibrations can travel. The Kwilu River people of Africa created a friction or humming drum by piercing the membrane covering the wooden body of the drum with a stick. The drummer would use a handful of wet leaves to grasp the stick inside the hollow body and slide his hand up and down to make the sound.

The Ancient Greeks had huge rowing boats called triremes. To help the rowers keep in time, a musician played two pipes made out of wood. The pipes were known as auloi and the musician was the aulete.

Pan-pipes

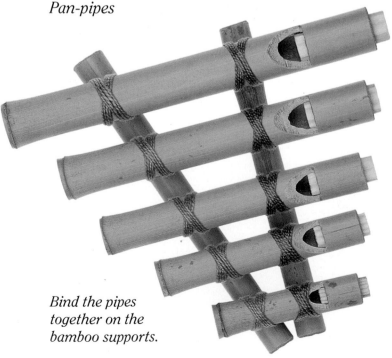

Bind the pipes together on the bamboo supports.

The Legend of Pan-pipes

Pan, the Greek god of shepherds, had the horns, ears and legs of a goat. He fell in love with the nymph, Syrinx, but she did not love him. Taking pity on Syrinx, the gods changed her into a reed. Pan cut a reed and made it into a pipe in memory of his lost love. Pan-pipes are traditional folk instruments, still played in China, Latin America and Europe, especially Romania. Recently, archaeologists discovered a set of Roman boxwood pan-pipes at Southwark, in London.

Making Pan-pipes

These pan-pipes are made from lengths of bamboo. Cut a 15 cm length of bamboo, with one end open, as shown here. Cut a notch in the bamboo about 3 cm from the open end. Plug the same end with a section of wood. Blow into the pipe and move the plug in and out until you have the best sound, then glue the plug in place. Make a set of pipes of different lengths and bind them together.

Cutting the Bamboo

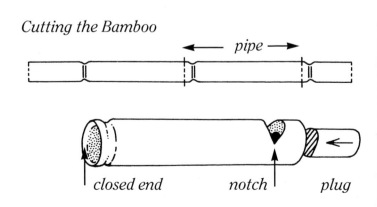

closed end   *notch*   *plug*

Rattles and Rasps

A rattle can be made by making holes in walnut shells and threading them on to a loop of wire. Alternatively, fill hollow gourds or coconuts with different seeds, Small light seeds give soft, whispery sounds. Heavier seeds and pods give a stronger rattle. A rasp is a wooden instrument in which grooves have been cut. Sticks are passed over the grooves making a rhythmic sound. Cut grooves in a piece of wood and make your own rasp.

Walnut Rattle

Rasp and Stick

Drumsticks

Drums and Xylophones

Banging one piece of wood with another must have made the first rhythmic sounds. Make a collection of branches and logs of various sizes and listen to the range of sounds that can be made by drumming them together. Can you create different notes? Does one wood make a higher sound than another? When you have experimented, make a xylophone with a range of notes. The sticks used to bang the instruments will also affect the sound. Try making a series of drumsticks using different materials.

Driftwood Xylophone

Glossary

amber A yellowish-brown resin that comes from ancient trees. It can be used for jewellery and ornaments.

carpenter A skilled craftsperson who makes objects from wood.

chlorophyll The green pigment in plants that traps the action of sunlight. Photosynthesis occurs and food is produced for the plant.

coppicing The practice of cutting the trunks of woodland trees close to the ground to encourage the fast growth of shoots.

deciduous Trees that shed their leaves each year in autumn.

ecosystem The group of animals and plants living in their environment.

environment The surroundings in which a plant or animal lives.

flexible A material that bends without breaking.

flora and fauna The plant and animal life of a particular place.

foliage The green parts of a plant.

food chain A community of families of living things dependent upon each other for food. Each feeds upon the family below in the chain.

grain The direction of the fibres in wood.

hardwoods Broad-leaved trees with strong, heavy wood, rather than the softwood produced by conifers.

horizontal Level or flat, parallel with the horizon.

knot A word that can mean a lump of plant tissue found on the trunk of a tree.

organic Relating to living things.

papier mâché A hard substance made from a pulp of paper and paste.

resonant A material that amplifies sound vibrations passing through it because it vibrates in sympathy.

sap The watery food circulating inside a plant.

sapling A young tree.

seasoned Wood that has been dried to make it suitable for use by a carpenter.

softwoods Coniferous trees with open-grained wood.

symmetry Similarity of shape about a given point or line.

tissue Animal or plant cells of the same kind.

vertical At right angles to the horizon – or upright.

More Information

Books to Read

Allen and Brown, *The Last Green Book on Earth?* Red Fox, 1994

Carlson, L. *EcoArt,* Williamson Publishing, 1993

Cochrane, J. *Trees of the Tropics*, Heinemann, 1990

Greenaway, T. *Fir Trees*, Heinemann, 1990

Greenaway, T. *Woodland Trees*, Heinemann, 1990

Petrash, C. *Earthwise*, Floris Books, 1993

Temple, L. *Dear World*, Bodley Head, 1994

Terzian, A. *The Kids' Multicultural Art Book*, Williamson Publishing, 1993

Written by Children of the World, *Rescue Mission Planet Earth – A Children's Edition of Agenda 21*, Kingfisher, 1994

Addresses for Information

Australia

Australian Conservation Foundation, 340 Gore Street, Fitzroy, VIC 3065

Canada

International Council for Local Environmental Initiatives, City Hall, East Tower, 8th Floor, Toronto Ontario M5H 2N2

UK

Friends of the Earth, 26-28 Underwood Street, London, N1 7JU

International Tree Foundation, Sandy Lane, Crawley Down, West Sussex, RH10 4HS

London Ecology Centre, 45 Shelton Street, Covent Garden, London, WC2 9HJ

Woodcraft Folk, 13 Ritherdon Road, London, SW17 8QE

Woodland Trust, Autumn Park, Dysart Road, Grantham, Lincs, NG31 6LL

Places to Visit (UK)

Natural History Museum, Cromwell Road, London, SW7

Museum of Mankind, Burlington Gardens, London, W1X 2EX

Sources for Special Materials

National Centre for Organic Gardening, Ryton-on-Dunsmore, Coventry, CV8 3LG

ECO-Haven, PO Box 214, Shrewsbury, Shropshire, SY1 2ZZ

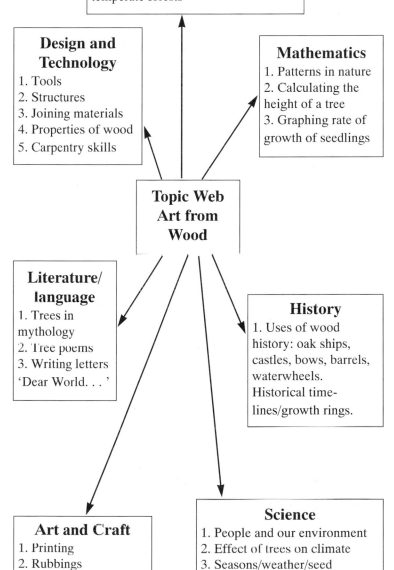

Geography
1. Location of forest types
2. Products from trees
3. Local study – tree survey
4. Lumbering/paper making industry/pollution/deforestation/rain forests/temperate forests

Design and Technology
1. Tools
2. Structures
3. Joining materials
4. Properties of wood
5. Carpentry skills

Mathematics
1. Patterns in nature
2. Calculating the height of a tree
3. Graphing rate of growth of seedlings

Topic Web Art from Wood

Literature/ language
1. Trees in mythology
2. Tree poems
3. Writing letters 'Dear World. . .'

History
1. Uses of wood history: oak ships, castles, bows, barrels, waterwheels. Historical time-lines/growth rings.

Art and Craft
1. Printing
2. Rubbings
3. Patterns
4. Pigments
5. Weaving
6. Collage
7. Making recycled paper

Science
1. People and our environment
2. Effect of trees on climate
3. Seasons/weather/seed dispersal
4. Ecosystems/habitats
5. Planting seeds, growing trees
6. Identifying trees
7. Making sounds/musical instruments made from wood

Index